User's Guide For Life

How to Discover Your Personal Vision and
Values and Then Apply Them to Your Life

Ray and Kathy Warren

Contents

Introduction

I couldn't help but notice some of the other fishermen grabbing their gear and quickly moving away from the river's edge. As I turned to find out what all the commotion was about, I noticed two young grizzly bear cubs quickly moving in to claim what some of the retreating fishermen left behind. The cubs' noses led them directly to the freshly caught red salmon that used to belong to those scrambling fishermen. So the bears began their feast, compliments of those nearby who knew better than to try and stop them, but who were watching helplessly as their morning's catch was devoured. This was probably the easiest fishing trip the young bears had experienced in a long time!

Watching intently from the edge of the trees was the large mother grizzly, ready to quickly intervene if she sensed any danger to her cubs. Needless to say the fishermen allowed plenty of room for the bears who easily took over these prime fishing spots until they were ready to move on down the river.

Here at the junction of the Kenai and the Russian Rivers is one of the best spots in Alaska to find salmon by the thousands, all making their way back to the very spot where they were born. At this point in their lives their sole purpose is to make it through the gauntlet of bears, fishermen, and any other predators, to reach their final destination, their spawning grounds further up the river.

Their first challenge had been down at the mouth of the magnificent Kenai, where commercial fishermen get the first crack at the teeming schools of fish, their fishing nets hauling in the abundant salmon as these fish leave their life in the ocean and begin their journey up the river. The next challenge had come farther upstream where the sports fishermen and the bears congregate every year to greet the arriving fish, whose rich red meat is some of the tastiest and most nutritious in the world.

So what in the world do wild Alaskan salmon have to do with this *User's Guide*? Is it just because we love to talk about the most beautiful and fascinating place in the world? That may be true, yet it's more than that. While exploring Alaska, we became enamored with the life of one of God's fascinating creatures. We soon realized that God was teaching us through the life of this fish, and we couldn't think of a better example to illustrate what we are going to talk about in the following sections than the **Alaska Salmon**.

God has placed in the salmon some unique qualities that we believe offer a picture of what a successful and fulfilling human life would include. From the day of their hatching these fish begin a journey that is both amazing and challenging. Though each salmon changes physiologically several times in its life, their **identity** is imprinted from birth. With a **vision** to pass on their **legacy** to the next generation, and focused on the **goal** of returning to the very same spawning ground they came from, every salmon struggles and fights with incredible tenacity to fulfill its **destiny.**

Salmon open our eyes to appreciate some strong **values**, such as perseverance, hard work, determination, steadfastness, and staying focused on the vision, to mention a few. Their final journey at the end of their lives is not easy; it's a one-way journey of *many* miles, swimming upstream against strong currents and over waterfalls, never stopping to eat along the way, escaping the myriads of fishermen, hungry bears, and other predators. Even when they finally arrive exhausted, they are still determined to secure a spawning nest before they spawn and die. The legacy is passed on into the new clusters of eggs, and these new salmon in turn will do the same as their parents.

In the same way, God has put in each one of His people a unique **destiny** that we alone can fulfill. And along with this unique destiny we are given, each of us will also play a key role in the overall master plan that God has ordained for His creation.

What is your life message?

A good question to ask when it comes to finding your destiny might be "what is my **life message**?" God has designed each person to be an expression of the message that He is communicating to mankind. So you might say that we each have a part of that message. Maybe you have never considered the fact that you are a living message. Wouldn't you like to know what He wants to speak through you? What will you do with your message? Will you be a faithful communicator of your message? Or will it stay hidden, kept only to yourself?

Fulfilling your destiny does not just happen by chance. Have you ever heard the old adage "If you aim at nothing, you are bound to hit it"? There certainly is a lot of truth in that old saying. Fulfilling your destiny will demand everything you've got (and truthfully, even that won't be enough; you will need God's help since it takes more than human ability and strength).

When a person first responds to God's call, he receives magnificent benefits. Yet along with those benefits comes a profound responsibility, for God has designed an eternal and unique destiny for each person to fulfill. We get to share in His divine purposes and plans for the world, which will bring ultimate glory to Him.

So you might now be asking, "If I have a divine destiny to fulfill, how do I know what that destiny is?" Well, that is one of the most critical questions every wise person seeks to answer. This *User's Guide* is an effort to help you discover the answer to that extremely important question, and to offer some tools to help you find and fulfill that destiny.

There is one critical subject that we will not be spending much time on here (we will later), but which is of the utmost importance. That is the fact that a person's whole life is based on what can be called a **belief system**. Your actions are a direct result of what you believe. If you try to live a fulfilling life without a true understanding of God and about life, then you are putting the cart before the horse. You see, this life is very short, and how you spend eternity will depend upon what your core beliefs are and how you live them out.

There are many belief systems in this world, but the one that we base *our* lives on is found in the life, death, and resurrection of Jesus Christ, the only Son of God. Jesus said that the only way for a person to have a relationship with God is through believing in Him and by the power of the Holy Spirit. We base our beliefs on the truths revealed in the Bible.

So where do you stand with God? There is no more important question that each person needs to answer in life. Again, how you answer that determines how and where you will spend eternity.

We wanted to be sure that we talked about what you believe before we ever started dealing with the subject of destiny since it is such a foundational and fundamental subject. So we are going to presuppose that you are settled on your beliefs and therefore can start moving toward your destiny.

What we hope to do in this *User's Guide* is to help you along on your life journey. This journey starts off with you clarifying your **identity and beliefs**. Then we will move on to finding and forming the **vision** that God has for your life. After identifying your personal vision, there will be a section in which we talk about some tools that can help you understand what your **core values** are. From there we will talk about how important it is for you to **set goals** and **make plans** to reach those goals.

By taking this process step by step, you will have a much better idea of where you are going in life and how to get there. In the final section we will talk about the importance of training the next generation to do the same thing; that is, how to pass along a **godly legacy** to future generations.

Got purpose?

Pastor Rick Warren wrote a book called *The Purpose Driven Life* which has broken records for its sales.[1] It is interesting to note that his book is all about fulfilling the **purpose**, or the destiny, God has for your life. We think one reason for this book's success is that deep down people instinctively long to live a life that has **purpose**.

As our American culture has drifted further and further away from God over the years, people are experiencing ever deeper longing for some sort of purpose. After all, having a purpose is directly tied to our **personal identity**. And having some sort of identity is one of the greatest and strongest longings of the human soul.

Rick Warren's book does a great job of painting a "macro" picture of finding purpose in life. What we want to do in this Guide is to help you find the "micro" picture of your life's purpose, and to supply you with what we have found to be some helpful tools for your life journey.

One day we will all stand before our Creator and we will be judged according to how we have lived our lives. The glory we are able to give Him, and our eternal rewards, will be determined by how we have passed our time here on earth. Our hope is that we all will receive the maximum reward, and hear those wonderful words from God found in Matthew 25:21 (NIV), "Well done, good and faithful servant! You have been faithful with a few things; I will put you in charge of many things. Come and share your Master's happiness!"[2]

---

[1] Rick Warren. *Purpose Driven Life*. Grand Rapids, Michigan: Zondervan (2002).

[2] Holy Bible. Matthew 25:21 New International Version (NIV).

We need to say one important thing about how this *User's Guide* is written. We are Christ-followers who believe that the Bible is the true word of God. Everything we do and believe is based on what God has written in the Scriptures. Even if you are not a Christ-follower as we are, we hope that you will still read this guide and benefit from it. If you consider yourself to be open-minded then you can still read this, even if you do not agree with some of our foundational beliefs.

We will be using a good number of quotes from the Bible. We will probably also make a number of statements without explaining that they came from the Bible and from our **Biblical worldview**. In our effort to keep this booklet very short and uncomplicated, we will not take the time to explain the background of many of these points. Thanks for giving us this liberty.

Leaving the past behind

There is another very important aspect to **fulfilling your destiny** that we need to mention before we get started moving forward. It is something that could keep you from ever making any forward progress in life. It has to do with the wounds, hurts, and negative issues that every person either inherits, experiences, or creates in life.

None of us had any choice about the family into which we were born. We did not choose our parents, grandparents, great-grandparents, etc. Yet the way our ancestors lived their lives has a tremendous effect on what kind of person we become. Maybe you came from a healthy family and had a wonderful upbringing. Yet even with the best possible childhood, we will probably have some unhealthy family patterns that need to be changed.

There are also **poor decisions** that we make in life which may result in anger, bitterness, guilt, disappointment, brokenness, disillusionment, resentment, etc. Although many times we would like to be able to change our past, we know that can't happen. Yet there *is* a healthy *leaving* **the past behind** that needs to take place. If we still have one foot stuck in the past, it will be extremely difficult to run the race before us. So as you begin your race of life, be sure to take the time and effort to get freed up from your past, freed from the baggage you brought into your race.

The Bible tells us about a man named Paul who persecuted God's people. When God showed him he had to change, Paul had to come to grips with his past. At that point he said, *"....Forgetting what is behind* and straining toward what is ahead, I press on toward the goal to win the prize for which God has called me..." Phil 3:13-14 (NIV)[3] (emphasis mine).

Thankfully for the Christ-follower, God has redeemed our past. In fact, the Bible says that when we began our walk with God, it was as if we were born into a totally new life. We read in 2 Cor. 5:17 (NLT)[4] "This means that anyone who belongs to Christ has become a new person. The old life is gone; a new life has begun!" So if God decides that our life is brand new, why shouldn't we let go of the past and leave behind regrets and sorrows?

Every person is born with a fallen human nature which is contrary to everything good and wholesome. This fallen nature is selfish, rude, twisted, rebellious, etc., and therefore it is the condition of our hearts that must be redeemed. Without this fallen nature being redeemed, everything we are writing about will only be of a very limited help to you.

God has set the believer free from this fallen nature through Jesus Christ. We have been redeemed to a new life, and now the old fallen nature is no longer our master! So there is no need to revert to letting that old nature hinder us from fulfilling our life's destiny. Now, through our Redeemer Jesus, we are FREE to run our race.

---

[3] Holy Bible, Philippians 3:13-14 New International Version (NIV).

[4] Holy Bible, 2 Corinthians 5: 17 New Living Translation (NLT).

Getting free from the past and overcoming our old evil nature are critical and necessary areas that need to be addressed before we can begin to pursue our destiny. However, this book will not go into these vast subjects; we will assume that you have already received some effective victory in these areas. If you try to begin your life race without having these areas dealt with for the most part, then you will be like a person trying to run a marathon with a broken leg. Who wants to try to run a race in that condition? Why not start off as a healthy runner?

An enemy you can't see

Let's not forget that there is an enemy of our souls who will try everything in his power to keep us from fulfilling our life's destiny. Before a person comes to Christ he is a slave to this enemy. Even after we come to Christ, there is still a battle to break out of this enemy's evil influence. His name is Satan, he is real, and he is God's arch enemy and therefore ours.

So there are two major enemies that must be overcome. One is our old evil human nature and the other is the devil and his demons. You can see why a person without Christ really has no hope for a truly victorious life since he has no power over either of these enemies. But God has provided a wonderful way for His people by defeating both of these adversaries for us, through Jesus Christ.

Over the years, my wife and I have had the privilege as counselors to be closely involved in the lives of a large number of people. We have had the opportunity to watch many people run their races. Some have gotten diverted, some have made big mistakes, and some have even quit their race altogether for a number of reasons. But others have followed hard after God and are running their races with determination and passion. Their aim is to cross the finish line a winner, receiving the prize that gives God the glory He deserves.

Our enemies never really give up; they will fight us throughout our entire lives. But we can be prepared for the fight. We must know the tactics of our adversaries. And all the while, as God's people, we know that through Jesus Christ, God has defeated our enemies. As we run the race He has marked out for us, He will give us the victory if we run with Him.

One more thing about finding freedom to run: this is a *lifelong process*. Our journey into wholeness and the fulfilling of our destiny go on throughout our lives. But we will find that as we grow in freedom our race will be easier to run. We should gain momentum throughout our lives so that by life's end we find ourselves sprinting to the finish line.

There's a passage in Hebrews 12:1 (NLT) that sums it all up:

"....let us strip off every weight that slows us down, especially the sin that so easily trips us up. And let us run with endurance the race God has set before us."[5]

So having said all that, let's jump into a few sections that contain tools we have found which we believe will help you. As we have personally discovered through our journey, it is wise to learn from others who are older and have gained valuable experience about how to succeed in this life!

Note:

It is very important that you work through each section one at a time and in order, as each section builds upon the preceding sections.

---

[5] Holy Bible. Heb. 12:1 New Living Translation (NLT).

Section 1:
Identity

"Become who you were born to be."
Elrond to Aragorn (*the future king of Gondor and Arnor*), in the movie
The Lord of the Rings: Return of the King.[6]

Every human being has a need deep down in the heart to find his or her true identity. The first question in life that we need to address is "Who am I?" The answer to this question determines much, not the least of which is why I am here, and where I am going....what my unique purpose is.

The story of Moses, found in the Bible, shows us how he came to grips with this question.

"Now Moses was keeping the flock of his father-in-law, Jethro, the priest of Midian, and he led his flock to the west side of the wilderness and came to Mt. Horeb, the mountain of God. And the angel of the Lord appeared to him in a flame of fire out of the midst of the bush. He looked, and behold, the bush was burning, yet it was not consumed. And Moses said, 'I will turn aside to see this great sight, why the bush is not burned.' When the Lord saw that he

---

[6] *Lord of the Rings: Return of the King,* dir. By Peter Jackson. Elijah Wood, Sean Astin, Orlando Bloom, Liv Tyler. Wingnut Films and The Saul Zaentz Company, distributed by New Line Cinema (2003). movie.

had turned aside to see, God called him out of the bush, 'Moses! Moses!' And he said, 'Here I am.' " (Exodus 3:1-4, ESV)[7]

Here we read the account of how God revealed Himself to Moses through an angel in order to assign to Moses the task of leading the nation of Israel out of the bondage of slavery in Egypt and into a land of promise, what the Bible calls a land of milk and honey. Moses was faithfully taking care of his father-in-law's sheep out in a lonely place, but God met him there and called him to a very challenging commission.

So there were two extremely important questions that Moses needed to have answered before he would be ready to carry out God's command:

- Who am I?
- Who is God?

Moses asked God, "**Who am I** that I should go to Pharaoh and bring the children of Israel out of Egypt?"(Exodus 3:11, ESV)[8] Moses realized that in his weakness as a simple shepherd there in the wilderness he was going to have to have a powerful word from God in order to be successful.

He got the answer when God said, "But I will be with you, and this shall be the sign for you, that I have sent you: when you have brought the people out of Egypt, you shall serve God on this mountain." (Exodus 3:12, ESV) [9] So God said in essence that from then on Moses was not just a man by himself, but **he was a man whom God promised to be with**. Moses became known and befriended by God. So that settled the first question about the new identity of Moses.

---

[7] Holy Bible. Exodus 3:1-4 English Standard Version (ESV).

[8] Holy Bible. Exodus 3:11, English Standard Version (ESV).

[9] Ibid.Exodus 3:12

The next critical question came when Moses asked God who He was.

He wanted to know what to say when the people of Israel ask him what God's name is; in other words, **who is God?** God said to tell them that (Exodus 3:14-15, ESV)[10] "I AM WHO I AM" sent him. He also said that He was "The Lord, the God of your fathers, the God of Abraham, the God of Isaac, the God of Jacob," and that He "has sent me to you." So that settled the second question about **who God is.**

This event happened several thousand years before Christ was on the earth; yet the same questions need to be answered by you today so that you can be very clear about your identity. You must know who God is and you must know who you are. Without these two questions being answered, no human being can know his or her true identity.

Every human being is born into this world with a sin nature. This means that every person is born a **slave** to sin, and suffers from the curses that accompany this spiritual darkness.

God, in His mercy, has made a way to set us free from this slavery and to come into His family as a child of God. This happens when we confess that we are sinners and accept Jesus Christ as our Savior and Lord.

Because of this our identity changes completely. From this time on our identity is found in Jesus Christ. We are no longer slaves but we are now sons and daughters of our Father God.

Becoming a child of God radically changes everything. Now, instead of living under the curse of sin, we have access to all the blessings that come with our new identity. We are no longer slaves but we are now free to know our Father God, and to live our lives in '

---

[10] Ibid. Exodus 3:14-15.

a joyful relationship with Him, fulfilling the purpose and destiny He has planned for us.

The focus of our lives is no longer directed toward ourselves and our own glory, but toward living an unselfish life focused on giving glory to God and caring more for others than for ourselves.

As believers in Christ, we know that our identity is firmly rooted in the fact that we were created by God and that He has a divine purpose for our lives. We know that He loves us with a perfect love and that He loved us before the world was even created. His love is so great for us, proven by the fact that He pursued us even when we were in sin and when we were not looking for Him.

Where else do people look?

The people without God are left to try to find some sort of **identity** from whatever source they can dream up. It is obvious today that many people are very confused about their identity. They are searching desperately for some sort of significance, but nothing on earth can satisfy this intrinsic and driving human need.

One of the most common beliefs today is that there is no God and **man is his own god**. Our Western culture generally teaches us that the existence of mankind and the universe happened by mere accident, that conditions just happened to exist which led to life, and this life happened to evolve over millions of years. Even though there has never been proof to substantiate this theory, it is taught as fact because any other explanation will not fit into the belief system of a world without God. This view of the world demands belief that human beings are not unique creations of God, but merely another life form a step or so above most animals.

So with that mindset, it logically follows that if the universe is only an accident and there is no God, then finding some meaningful personal **identity** and **purpose** in life will prove to be difficult. It means that you can concoct most any identity you want,

18

whatever works for you. It also means that there is no way to truly determine what is right and what is wrong, since man is his own god and man is the measure of all things. Everyone can come up with his own view of morals and beliefs. The result is utter confusion and chaos, the very things we see so rampant in our world today.

The only problem with this mindset is that there *is* a God, He is very real and very personal, and He has made it clear that there are absolute rights and wrongs. He made the universe in order to reveal His glory and He will hold all people accountable for how they live their lives on the earth.

The more we get to know God, the more we know about who we are. Then we can find out what specific purpose God had for creating us and putting us on this earth. As we said earlier, He has a **specific destiny** for each one of us that He wants us to find and fulfill. In the following sections we will learn more about how to find, pursue, and fulfill that destiny.

Section 2:
Central Beliefs

At the beginning of the 1900s, the Boxer Rebellion broke out in China. As a result the new rulers wanted to rid the land of foreigners, including most all of the Christian missionaries who were living there. A large number of these missionaries sought refuge from this slaughter by gathering at the compound of the Shansi governor. But he unexpectedly threw them in prison and then quickly decided to have them all executed.

Years later one of the executioners described the scene as the prisoners were brought out and lined up to be killed. He had watched husbands and wives turn and kiss each other and their children. They pointed to heaven and began singing as the executioners ended their lives. This executioner was so impacted by the faith and fearlessness of the missionaries that he later gave his life to Christ. He could see from their example that they truly believed in something beyond this life and were empowered through their **belief** to face the worst. (From an article in Ruth Bell Graham's writings called "Ruth's Attic".) [11]

---

[11] Graham, Ruth Bell. "Ruth's Attic: Harvest from Tragedy". Paraphrased from a *Decision* (Billy Graham Evangelistic Association) magazine. Date and issue unavailable.

What do you believe?

Once you have found and are assured of your true identity, then it is vital that you discover and become established in your **belief system** (sometimes called your **worldview**). Your beliefs form the foundation for your **convictions**, which are those things you are willing to give your time, talent, money, and life for.

You can break down a belief system into three parts:

1. **What you believe about God**

2. **What you believe about yourself**

3. **What you believe about other people and the world around you**

In today's world, many people would say that all belief has to be based on what a person can access through the five senses. This means that they must believe only what they can prove by observing and experiencing things in the natural world. They would probably agree with the statement which says **"seeing is believing."**

But what if there *is* a spiritual world that cannot be seen or experienced by the natural senses alone? What if there *is* a Creator God who cannot be seen, yet rules both the spiritual world and the natural world, and who will hold all people accountable one day for how they have lived their life on earth? People who believe this way could say **"believing results in true seeing."**

There are crucial questions which every person must answer. How they answer them determines their belief system, which then determines how they live their life on earth.

A May 2017 George Barna poll on the topic of world view shows that only around 17 per cent of those who call themselves active Christians have a Biblical world view.[12] Another Barna poll showed that only about half of Christian ministers hold a Biblical worldview![13] So we see that there is a huge gap between a truly Biblical worldview and what many Christians believe.

We have put an example of a **Biblical belief statement** at the end of this *User's Guide* (Appendix) so you can see how your beliefs compare and hopefully you can put together a statement of your own. Your belief system is something you must grapple with and immerse yourself in if you are going to be an effective example of a true Christ-follower. One way to get to know God better is to get to know His attributes (His personality, His character, etc.). One of the ways you can do this is by reading a good theology book, such as Wayne Grudem's *Systematic Theology*,[14] for a clear understanding of the nature of God.

We encourage you to look at the belief statements of churches that you respect, and then develop your own personal statement. Immerse yourself in your belief statement until it becomes your conviction. Then as you walk it out in your life, you can impart it to your family and to others.

---

[12] Barna, George.*Competing Worldviews Influence Today's Christians.* May 9, 2017. Retrieved Dec.16, 2017 from "Research Releases" in "Culture and Media", www.barna.com/research/competing-worldviews-influence-today's-Christians.

[13] Barna, George. *Only Half of Protestant Pastors Have a Biblical Worldview.* Jan. 12, 2004. Retrieved Dec. 16, 2017 from "Articles" in "Leaders and Pastors", www.barna.com/research/only-half-of-Protestant   -pastors-have-a-Biblical-worldview.

[14] Grudem, Wayne. *Systematic Theology.* Grand Rapids, Michigan: Zondervan, 1994.

Section 3:

Vision

"Vision without action is a daydream; action without vision is a nightmare."
Old Japanese proverb[15]

On the barren sand dunes of North Carolina's coast, the dream was finally fulfilled. Just a very few years into the 1900s, two brothers from Ohio put together their many different ideas and discoveries to create this final product. It had taken years of experimentation, study, research, perseverance, and just plain hard work to get to this point. Now was the moment of truth; would it be a success, or just a lot of work and expense for nothing?

Very few people in that day had ever even imagined such a thing, much less tried to bring it into reality. Only a true visionary-type person could see into the future when people would travel from place to place in a motorized aircraft.

But here they were on the verge of making history. They did not have the backing of the government or some deep-pocketed corporation. They did not have anyone's footsteps to follow since it had never before been done. There were no crowds around to cheer

---

[15] Krieger, Richard Alan. *Civilization's Quotations: Life's Ideal* (2002), p.280. Algora Publishing, www.algora.com.

them on. There was no one to encourage them when they had crashes, equipment failures, and other setbacks. In fact, after one failed attempt Wilbur Wright had even stated that he knew men would fly but doubted that it would happen in his lifetime!

But it did happen. Orville Wright won the coin toss to be the first to give it a try. So on that cold December day in 1903, the first motor-powered manned flight of its kind took place. It was a small step in one way since the flight only covered a distance of around 120 feet, but it was a huge step, a monumental step in the beginning of aeronautical history. Before the end of Orville's life in 1948 the world was on the verge of supersonic flight; how amazing!

In the beginning of Andy Stanley's book entitled *Visioneering*,[16] he mentions the vision-birthing event which spurred on Orville and Wilbur Wright and so impacted the course of history. Their father had brought home a rubber band-powered toy that resembled a helicopter, and released it into the air right in their home. When the boys saw this whirling device rise into the air on its own, they were captivated by the whole idea of flight, and right there the vision was birthed, a vision that never left them as they grew up.

After hearing about other pioneers who were experimenting with aviation ideas and reading most all that was available on the subject (and there wasn't much at the time), they began their own quest to fulfill their dream to fly. The vision in their hearts would be tried and tested many times before the day of victory finally arrived. Yet once they had tasted the thrill of flight, they soon sold their bicycle repair shop in order to devote themselves totally to their passion for flying and improving their aeronautical inventions.

---

[16] Stanley, Andy. *Visioneering*. Sisters, Oregon: Multnomah Publishing, Inc. 1999.

What is your vision?

The big question for each person is this: What is the primary vision that is in *your* heart? What gets you motivated and releases passion in *you*? What is the subject that you love to talk about? What are you willing to spend your time and money on? It may not seem to be as monumental and world-changing as the vision of the Wright brothers, but that is not the point. The important thing is that you discover the vision that God has planned for *your* life and fulfill that vision. It goes beyond the temporary and has eternal significance.

What is the driving force behind how you make your decisions and how you live your life? Does your vision reach beyond just the next month or the next year? And where did you get your vision? Is it from reading or hearing about someone else's life? Maybe you have never really given much thought to vision and have never really tried to put into writing your own personal vision statement.

There is a verse in the Bible that says, "Where there is no vision, the people are unrestrained, but happy is he who keeps the law." (Prov. 29:18, NASB)[17] One of the main purposes of our lives is to find out what God is doing on the earth and then go out and fulfill our part in that great vision. Only then will we be fulfilled and find true joy in life.

In the story *Alice in Wonderland* by Lewis Carroll,[18] Alice came to a fork in the road and she asked the Cheshire Cat in the tree for directions:

---

[17] Holy Bible. Proverbs 29:18. New American Standard Version (NASB).

[18] Carruth, Jane. *Alice in Wonderland Quotes*. Retrieved December 14, 2017 from *Alice in Wonderland Quotes* by Jane Carruth-Goodreads>work>2933712-alice-in-wonderland.

Alice: Would you tell me, please, which way I ought to go from here?

Cat: That depends a good deal on where you want to get to.

Alice: I don't much care where....

Cat: Then it doesn't matter which way you go.

Alice: ......so long as I get somewhere.

Cat: Oh, you're sure to do that, if only you walk long enough.

So many people are like Alice, walking through life with no vision for their lives. They can travel great distances along their life journey; but if they have no vision, no direction, they have no idea where their journey is headed and may end up where they never wanted to be. Indeed, because the humanistic philosophy of the day teaches us that we human beings are no different than animals, we come along steeped in the erroneous belief that our individual lives have no purpose. Engraved in many minds is the belief that there is nothing unique about us, that we are not God's special creation. No wonder so many people today just seem to aimlessly drift through life!

If someone were to ask you today to tell him what your life's vision is, what would you say? Did you know that every decision you make determines where you are going in life? Most of life is made up of many small decisions which, when combined, add up to be very important as a whole.

When people are young they seldom think about the long-term impact of their lives. Most young people are just excited about getting to the next birthday. But when people grow older they begin to take time to reflect on how they have used their years. Some can be very satisfied realizing they had some positive impact on the world, while others are plagued by regret about how they lived and how little their lives amounted to. There is also the most important factor to consider: how we spend our years in this life will determine how we will spend eternity. What could be more important than that?

How do you find your vision?

So how do you find the vision for *your* life? Should you try to emulate some person that you admire? Should you look around at what others do and then try to pick something out for yourself? Or will you let someone else determine your vision for you?

Actually you don't have to go very far to find it, because when you were created God put a vision right inside your heart. Each person has been uniquely equipped with a special DNA that is unlike anyone else in the world. This is true biologically for our physical body; it is also true that God has given each of us a non-physical "DNA" which is His unique plan for our life. There is a message inside you that needs to be communicated to the world. Will your message be like the proverbial "message in a bottle" that drifts through the oceans and ends up on a deserted island never to be found or read?

In this passage from the Bible (Proverbs 4:23, 25-27, NIV)[19] the writer talks about how vision is connected to the heart. "Above all else, **guard your heart**, for everything you do flows from it. Let your eyes **look straight ahead**; fix your gaze directly before you. Give **careful thought** to the paths for your feet and be steadfast in all your ways. Do not turn to the right or to the left; **keep your foot from evil**." (emphasis mine)

We can see from this passage that all aspects of life start with what's in the heart, and we also understand that there is a danger that we can be distracted from the vision and not end up where we want to be. In these verses it is obvious that the author is not just talking about a physical heart and a natural pathway. Here the "eyes" are

---

[19] Holy Bible. Proverbs 4:23, 25-27. New International Version (NIV).

referring to vision that is within a person, vision of the heart. And the pathway is the road of a person's life journey.

There is an interesting quote from Tolkien's *Lord of the Rings* where Frodo's uncle, Bilbo Baggins, says, "It's a dangerous business going out of your door. You step into the road, and if you don't keep your feet, there is no knowing where you might be swept off to." [20]

There is a lot of truth in Bilbo's words. If a person has no clear vision for where he is going, he might just get swept away to a place he does not want to go.

Even after we find a clear vision it is possible to be sidetracked by life's distractions and not stay true to that vision. The human tendency is to get excited about the novelty of a new-found life vision. But as we begin to walk out that vision and face obstacles and difficulties, we tend to lose focus, get sidetracked, or even drop the vision altogether.

As we can see through the example of the Wright brothers, we can't fulfill our vision from our easy chairs. There is a price to pay, which can take the form of risk and sacrifice. It will require courage, confidence, commitment, and perseverance.

"Write the vision, and make it plain on tablets, so he may run who reads it." (Habakkuk 2:2, ESV)[21]

Until you get it down in writing, your vision will probably seem ethereal and elusive. Once it's put down in writing, you can get your hands around it and begin to let it bring direction to your life. So how do you go about trying to write out a vision statement (sometimes called a mission statement)?

---

[20] *Lord of the Rings: Fellowship of the Ring.* Peter Jackson. Elijah Wood, Sean Astin, Orlando Bloom, Liv Tyler. Wingnut Films, Saul Zaentz Company, distributed by New Line Cinema. (2001). Movie.

[21] Holy Bible. Habakkuk 2:2. English Standard Version (ESV).

Great tool for writing down your vision

A friend gave us a copy of a great article called "Finding Your Focus" by Adam Holz,[22] which we found to be a real help in creating a vision statement. Through answering the following questions (from his article, with some of our own added in) you can start putting your statement together. Be sure to **write down** your answers because it is very important to see them written out.

- What are you passionate about?

- What are your primary strengths?

- What are your biggest weaknesses?

- In your work experiences, at what have you excelled? What have you struggled with the most?

- Which of your achievements have given you the greatest satisfaction?

- What are your primary gifts and talents? (There are a number of good gifts tests you can take to determine your gifts.)

- What have you learned about yourself as you have exercised your gifts?

- Ask two or three people who are close to you how they would describe your strengths, weaknesses, and passions.

---

[22] Holz, Adam, Finding Your Focus." *Discipleship Journal*, NavPress. Issue 121, 2001. www.navpress.com. Used by permission from NavPress, the Navigators (retrieved Dec. 18, 2017).

- How have your friends' perceptions of you shed new light on the way God has wired you?

- List your main talents. (Don't be bashful; you have some!)

- What action words would you choose to describe what you love to do? For example: draw, sing, counsel, build, travel, etc.....list as many as you can think of. Then pick two or three that best capture what you enjoy.

- How would you describe your personality? Do your personal strengths and weaknesses give you any clues about what you might pursue, or definitely should not pursue, as a life mission?

- Imagine your life ten years from now. What would you like to have accomplished? Consider the question in terms of the major areas of your life: key relationships, career, education, ministry, finances, and so on.

- What do you most enjoy doing in your free time? Why?

- Imagine that you had all the money you needed for the next ten years and didn't have to work. What would you do? Where would you go? Who would you want to be with?

- Think about some of the deepest disappointments you have experienced. What have they taught you about how God has wired you?

- At your funeral, what would you like for people to say about you? What do you want to be remembered for the most?

- Which people in history do you most admire and why? Which of their characteristics would you like to emulate?

And the following questions are for people of faith:

- What Biblical passages has God used deeply in your life? What is your favorite passage? What is your favorite book in the Bible?

- How have these scriptures shaped your view of life and the world?

- How has God used you in the past?

- What people in the Bible do you most admire and want to be like?

- What directional or prophetic words have you received (that have been confirmed and that you have a strong witness to)?

Reread your answers to the questions.

1. Do you have any new insights into how God has designed you? Write them down.

2. What themes are repeated in your answers to the questions?

3. What ideas excited you the most as you wrote them down?

4. Did any of the questions cause something to click in your mind and make you say "That's what I need to do."?

5. Write down the phrases that capture your most important discoveries from this process. Begin with simple sentences that describe specific actions, such as "I really like working with my hands". Don't feel pressured to come up with your final and complete statement right away. If after an hour or two you're struggling to know what to write, put your notes away and return to them in a day or two, or even next week.

Eventually you will be able to put together a short vision statement. It should express what you were created for, why you are on this earth, and where you are going in life. It needs to be short and concise, something you can pretty easily remember.

Don't worry about trying to get it perfect all at once. You will probably have to spend a lot of time thinking this through, trying to create something that you are happy with. Most likely it will be something you continue to work on, giving time to let it sit before going back over it again to see if it needs to be adjusted or tweaked, or even rewritten.

After all, developing your personal vision is a life-long process; it will not be fully developed all at once. In fact, you will find that your vision statement will develop progressively over time as you begin to see more and more clearly the pathway of your life journey.

Wayne Gretzky, one of the most famous hockey stars to ever play the game, was once asked why he thought he'd been such a record-holding success. His answer was relatively simple. He responded that "a good hockey player plays where the puck **is**; a great hockey player plays where the puck **is going to be**." In other words, Wayne Gretzky skated toward his vision.[23]

---

[23] Gretzky, Wayne. *Wayne Gretzky Quotes,* BrainyQuote.com. Retrieved December 12, 2017.

Section 4:
Values

One of our favorite parts of J.R.R. Tolkien's trilogy, *Lord of the Rings*, is when Mr. Frodo is ready to give up on his dangerous mission to destroy the ring. His faithful helper, Samwise Gamgee, steps up with a great burst of encouragement:

Frodo: I can't do this, Sam.

Sam: I know. It's all wrong. By rights we shouldn't even be here. But we are. It's like in the great stories, Mr. Frodo. The ones that really mattered. Full of darkness and danger, they were. And sometimes you didn't want to know the end. Because how could the end be happy? How could the world go back to the way it was when so much bad had happened? But in the end, it's only a passing thing, this shadow. Even darkness must pass. A new day will come. And when the sun shines it will shine out the clearer. Those were the stories that stayed with you. That meant something, even if you were too small to understand why. But I think, Mr. Frodo, I do understand. I know now. Folk in those stories had lots of chances of turning back, only they didn't. They kept going. Because they were holding on to something.

Frodo: What are we holding on to, Sam?

Sam: That there is some good in this world, Mr. Frodo…**and it is worth fighting for**. [24]

Sam is reminding Mr. Frodo of the many stories of those in the past who had not given up on their life mission. He says that the reason they did not turn back was because they had something good that they **valued** so much, it was worth fighting for. Those people were "holding on to something."

Most people have something they value enough to fight for, as opposed to simply having preferences which are not that important. Something worth fighting for, a conviction, would be something that they place a high **value** on. What are your personal values? What are the values that you would be willing to fight for? What would you consider important enough to pay a high price for? These are questions each of us should consider and think about. The answers will lead us to discover our own core values. They are a determining factor in our developing relationships; a person usually ends up spending time and making relationships with people of like values. In fact, if a person tries to connect with another person or group of people who do not share the same values, eventually there will be division of some sort.

Aubrey Malphurs has written a great book on values called *Values-Driven Leadership*.[25] In this book he describes values to be like the motor of a car and vision to be like the steering wheel. He makes his point of how important values are. A car with a great steering wheel but no motor would be useless.

---

[24] *Lord of the Rings:Return of the King.*Peter Jackson. Elijah Wood, Sean Astin, Orlando Bloom, Liv Tyler. WingNut Films, Saul Zaentz Company, New Line Cinema (2003). Movie.

[25] Malphurs, Aubrey. *Values-Driven Leadership.* Grand Rapids, Michigan: Baker Books, 1996, 2002.

The importance of your personal values

He says that people are **vision-focused, but values-driven**. Values are what give us the motivation to live life. Vision keeps a person moving in a certain direction but values are what give the drive to get to the destination. So you can see how important a person's values really are. If there is a deficiency of either vision or values then the person will never completely fulfill his or her life's destiny.

Vision dictates **where** we are going; values answer **why** we are going. To have a lot of vision without the right values to propel you along toward your goal could leave you just being a dreamer. Dreamers are those who are full of wonderful ideas, yet are seldom able to see any of those dreams fulfilled. There is absolutely nothing wrong with dreaming. In fact, great accomplishments start with dreams. But a dream by itself is usually just a fantasy.

Everyone has a set of values, even if they have never been aware of what those values are. But if you were to examine their lives you would eventually be able to make a list of what their values are. How do they spend their money? How do they spend their time? What do they count as important in life? What do they get excited about? What makes them happy or sad?

Some people put a high value on gourmet food. They would be willing to spend large sums of money at the grocery store or in restaurants to get just the right food to eat. Others would consider that to be excessive. It all depends upon the person's values.

One person will put a high value on relationships with certain people resulting in spending large amounts of time with them. Maybe you remember when you first fell in love with that special someone. You were probably willing to spend every waking moment with that person if you could have done so. You really placed a high value on that relationship, and the time you spent on it reflected that.

As a counselor and pastor, I (Ray) have done a lot of pre-marital counseling. One of my goals in this type of counseling is to find out if the two people have the same **basic values**, because in the long run this will eventually make or break a marriage. Even though it may seem difficult to end an engagement, it would never compare to the pain and heartache they would have experienced if they had gotten married and then later had to deal with irreconcilable differences.

Can you see why it is so important to know what your values are? Once you have your values written out so you can see them clearly, you might find that some really need to be changed. Or you might find that you are in the wrong job, in the wrong church, or in wrong relationships.

While some values seem to be a part of us from a very young age, most are what we learn from those around us. Children will usually take on the values of their families and friends. They learn values over the years by experience. One of the greatest responsibilities of parents is to train children to have healthy and godly values. This takes a concerted and consistent effort.

Therefore it is not enough for parents to merely be an example of good values to their children. It takes training and reinforcement for children to learn. Sadly, today most children are not being adequately trained but are left to themselves to take on the values of their culture. This usually ends up being the cause of great loss and difficulty for them through their entire lives.

Once a healthy set of values is established, then we must endeavor to live by them. They should act as a guide to keep us on track, and they will reflect what God has called us to do with our lives. Different people can have different values and that does not necessarily make one right and another wrong.

We can give you an example from our own life. Knowing early on in our marriage that we were called to plant churches, we realized that we needed to structure our lives in such a way that would enable us to survive the challenges that church planters face. We knew that there would be many times when we would not have an adequate income and sometimes no church income at all.

So early on we knew one of the values we would have to adopt would be that of a simple and frugal lifestyle. Part of this plan would require us to live a life owing no debts to anyone. As we were reading some very good material written by a Christian financial expert, we were impressed by a statement he made which said that it was possible and very important to pay off all your debts as quickly as you can so you could live debt free.

The thought of being completely free of debt had never entered our minds! It seemed so far out of the range of possibility that we were not able to imagine it, much less begin to take steps to see that brought to reality. But after reading that article and discussing it, we both agreed that this should be one of our values. So we prayed and began to plan.

After adopting a plan and following it diligently over a number of years, we were able to become debt free, including having no mortgage on our home. We accomplished this several years before our son went off to college. And since we had no debts, we were also able to pay for his education without him taking out any loans. So he graduated with no college loans to pay back as he started his career. What a blessing for him and for us!

A few years earlier, while our son was still in high school, our church sent us out to plant a church in another community. We were able to survive those early years when the young church was not able to give us any financial support. If we had had debts (like car loans, a home loan, credit card debt, etc.) we would have had a hard time making ends meet.

So in our case a simple and frugal lifestyle was a very critical value to have. Maybe someone else is called to be a successful business person, able to make a lot of money and relate to people in those circles. They would have to adopt a lifestyle that is not as simple and frugal like ours in order to do so. But they would still need to adopt a lifestyle with values that would enable them to fulfill what God had called them to do.

Below are two parables Jesus spoke concerning values in the 13th chapter of the book of Matthew (emphasis mine):

"The kingdom of heaven is like what happens when someone finds a treasure hidden in a field and buries it again. A person like that is happy and goes and sells everything in order to buy that field."

"The kingdom of heaven is like what happens when a shop owner is looking for fine pearls. After finding a very **valuable one**, the owner goes and sells everything in order to buy that pearl." (Matt.13:44-45 CEV)[26]

Here Jesus is teaching about how important it is for us to set the Kingdom of Heaven as that which we value most highly. In fact, it is so precious that He tells us to set its value above everything else in this life - quite a challenge! He taught us that the source of all true and eternal treasure is found in the Kingdom of God.

In both parables we see a very good picture of what it means to truly **value** something. Both seekers put a very high value on what they had discovered. They sold everything they owned in order to be able to purchase the treasure they had found.

It is very important that we write down our values. Until we write them down we really don't have a clear understanding of what they are.

How do you identify your values?

You can do a personal values audit by using the tool below. You will find a list of 58 personal values. Some of these came from Malphurs' book, *Values-Driven Leadership*, [27]and some from our

[26] Holy Bible. Matthew 13:44-45. Contemporary English Version (CEV).

[27] Malphurs, Aubrey. *Values-Driven Leadership*. Grand Rapids, Michigan: Baker Books, 1996, 2002.

life experiences. Read over the list and rate each one on a scale of 1 to 10, 1 being not very important and 10 being most important.

Remember, for this to be valid you must only rate them according to what they actually are in your life in the present (**actual values**), not what you would like for them to be (**aspired values**). You can also make a separate list of your **aspired values** that you can work on for the future.

You want to end up with around six or eight values that are 10s. The rest will be sprinkled out as 9s and on down to 1s. You may also have values that are not on this list. Simply add them in on the blanks at the bottom of the list.

1. Efficiency

2. Creativity and Innovation

3. Unity

4. Dependence on God

5. Strong Marriage

6. Strong Family

7. Simplicity

8. Financial Responsibility

9. Friendliness

10. Orderliness

11. Prayer and Devotional Life

12. Character and Integrity

13. Discipleship

14. Fellowship

15. Time Management

16. Success

17. Strong Work Ethic

18. Frugality

19. Comfortable Lifestyle

20. Accountability

21. Responsibility

22. Healthy Self-Image

23. Acceptance

24. Giving and Tithing

25. Quality Education

26. Using Spiritual Gifts

27. Being Debt Free

28. Loyalty

29. Faithfulness

30. Servanthood

31. Courage

32. Freedom

33. Informality

34. Separated from the World

35. Holiness and Purity

36. Good Name/Reputation

37. Social Justice

38. Flexibility

39. Truth and Truthfulness

40. Kingdom of God

41. Grace Mindset

42. Godly Children

43. Foreign Missions

44. Commitment

45. Submission

46. Biblically-principled Life

47. Sanctification

48. Physical Exercise

49. Healthy Diet

50. Travel

51. Mercy

52. Available to the Lord

53. Excellence

54. Leisure and Recreation

55. Evangelism

56. Close Personal Relationships

57. Hospitality

58. Worship

59. _____

60. _____

61. _____

62. _____

63. _____

Tally up your list and group them according to your numbered ratings. Now you have a better understanding of what is important to you. You might be very happy with your results or you may see that you need to make some changes. There might be some 2s that should be much higher up on the scale and there might be some 9s that should be 2s. After completing this survey, not only will you be more aware of your own values, but you will be able to better recognize the values of others as well.

Now you can make a values' statement according to your results. Make sure that your values match up well with your vision statement. For example, if your vision statement is leading you into a lifestyle where you will not have a large or dependable income, then the value of **frugality** and **simplicity of life** should be very important to you. Or if you are heading into a life calling that requires a high degree of physical demands you will want to be sure that **exercise** and **healthy lifestyle** are high on your values list.

Once you have established a healthy set of values, then you should try your best to live by them. Remember the picture of a car, **the steering wheel being like our vision and the motor being like our values**. Our values should act as a motivation to keep us moving along the road toward fulfilling our life vision.

Section 5:
Goals and Planning

"A goal without a plan is just a wish."
Antoine de St. Exupery[28]

The oversized wheels of the bush plane bounced along the rocky Arctic tundra as we touched down for our landing. Before long we had unloaded all our gear and the pilot fired up his engines to make the return flight back to the Inupiat (Eskimo) village of Kotzebue, hopefully before the strong winds kicked up again to make his homeward flight and landing more of a challenge. What a strange feeling it was to watch the plane disappear into the distance, realizing we were all alone now; just us and the grizzlies, wolves, caribou, and the other wild animals out there on the tundra.

It had finally come true! I (Ray) could hardly believe this was really happening! Since my teen years I had dreamed of going big game hunting in Alaska, and now here I was experiencing my dream. On top of that, I was with my son Andrew, and his best friend Pete. The three of us had done a number of wilderness trips to other places in the past; now we were getting ready to do my biggest one ever! Andrew had been living in Alaska for some time and had learned how to camp and hunt safely in the unforgiving wilderness.

---

[28] St. Exupery, Antoine de. Classical Quotes, #34212. Retrieved December 12, 2017 from www.quotationspage.com.

His friend Pete is also an accomplished outdoorsman, so we had enough experience and hunting savvy to make it a great trip. A few years prior the two of them had done a hunt much like this one and had learned some lessons the hard way. We would now benefit from many of the things they had learned.

This trip was a great success in all ways, but that did not happen by accident. It took a lot of **planning** and **preparation** to be sure we had the right types of shelter, clothing, food, and equipment, and also that we would be in the right place to find some caribou. Our **goal** was to have a safe and enjoyable trip, and for each of us to bring back a nice caribou with an equally nice set of antlers. This is not always easy to accomplish in the vast and sometimes dangerous Arctic wilderness. (In fact, at the end of our hunt on the way back to the base camp, we talked with some other hunters who had taken no game, and others who suffered serious equipment failures....not a good thing out in the Alaskan wilderness!)

Many months prior to the trip we had put our heads together to plan. Where would we go, how would we get there, and what equipment would we need to bring? On their previous trip to this same place Andrew and Pete's tent had been destroyed by the fierce Arctic winds that can whip across the tundra, leaving them to sleep without a tent, wrapped in loose tarps. So this time we rented a professional expedition-grade tent from our outfitter. Even so, one night the cold wind and rain were so violent that we thought our tent would surely disintegrate like theirs had before. But this time it held up thanks to the good planning and learning from their former experience.

Another precaution we took was to rent a global satellite phone so we could communicate with our bush pilot back at the village if an important need arose. And it just so happened that our first hunt site proved unproductive so we called in and had our pilot fly out and move us to another location which proved to be a much more productive site. Needless to say we were very glad we had thought to bring the global phone so we could make contact with our pilot.

Feeling quite certain that we would get some caribou, we had to make a plan to store hundreds of pounds of freshly dressed caribou meat and not have it stolen by hungry bears. We were careful to wrap our dressed meat in tarps and then store it far enough away from camp so that at night we would not find ourselves caught between an aggressive grizzly and our cache of fresh meat. Of course, we were careful to stay armed and loaded throughout the nights. Thankfully we never had to deal with any marauding bears or wolves and we never had to face the decision of whether or not to challenge hungry animals in the dark of night for the sake of our treasured meat.

For the better part of the next year we enjoyed caribou steaks and sausage, and we are still enjoying the pictures and memories we brought back from our hunt. Our success and safety were largely due to the meticulous **planning** we had done beforehand. We had prepared in advance for unexpected surprises, dangers, and the challenges of a sometimes hostile environment, which enabled us to have the experience of a lifetime which we will always fondly remember.

All three of us had the **vision** for this trip. And we had put a high **value** on having a safe and fruitful hunt. But if we had not done thorough **planning** it is doubtful that our trip would have been nearly as successful.

Does God make plans?

In Proverbs 21:5 (NIV) we read, "The plans of the diligent lead to profit as surely as haste leads to poverty".[29] In other words, if we avoid the temptation to skip over the planning process then we greatly improve our chances for success. There is a very well-known quote, often attributed to Benjamin Franklin, on the subject of

---

[29] Holy Bible. Proverbs 21:5. New International Version (NIV).

planning that goes like this: **"If you fail to plan, you are planning to fail."**[30]

Again in the book of Jeremiah we read, "For I know the plans I have for you, declares the Lord, plans for welfare and not for evil, to give you a future and a hope." (Jer. 29:11, ESV)[31] Here we see that God Himself makes plans, and He has made plans for us as individuals. So wouldn't it be really wise on our part to find out what those plans are? This passage says that He wants to prosper us and give us hope and a bright future; what a great blessing that is!

If we make plans that originate from our own minds without God's direction, we are planning in vain. Again in the book of Proverbs this is spelled out very clearly (Prov. 19:21, ESV): "Many are the plans in the mind of man, but it is the purpose of the Lord that will stand."[32] We want to be sure that our plans are in line with His plans so we can have true eternal success, not just something temporary. In the end God's plans will prevail!

Picture in your mind what a house constructed with no plans would look like. To begin with, it would be unsafe to even walk into a house like that! When you look at the lives of people who don't plan, you can see evidence of some very similar characteristics: confusion, anxiety, fear, financial lack, chaos, stress and worry, etc.

It is not uncommon to run across people having financial problems. What we have found is that many of these issues are rooted in lack of self-control **and lack of planning**. When people would ask for help, we could give them the tools and the counsel they needed, and they would usually agree that they needed to make some changes. But after time had passed many would still be stuck

---

[30]   Benjamin   Franklin>Quotes>Quotable   Quotes.   Goodreads.com; goodreads>quotes>#460142-if-you-fail-to-plan-you-are-planning-to-fail.   Retrieved December 12, 2017.

[31] Holy Bible. Jeremiah 29:11. English Standard Version (ESV).

[32] Holy Bible. Proverbs 19:21. ESV.

in their same problems because they failed to change their lifestyle, or to begin doing some planning. After all, a budget is simply a financial **plan.**

Let me give you an example of a goal our family set many years ago. We really felt that it was important for us and especially for our son to have the opportunity to travel a great deal in order to increase our understanding of people and cultures in other areas of our United States as well as in other countries. So we began to discuss where we should go, and we set some goals to help us accomplish our travels. Naturally this affected the financial side of our planning, but it had to start with us first making certain travel goals.

One year we decided to drive/camp across the U.S. Before we ever left town Kathy had researched the different states we were going to travel through along our route. She gathered information and studied different travel books pertaining to every state we would visit. We wanted to be sure we would not miss any of the unique parks, sites, and landmarks along the way, especially those with historical importance and those not visible from the main highways.

For several years afterwards we visited different parts of the U.S., being especially careful to take in all the historical sites we could find. We were able to visit most of the lower 48 states over the years. Later on when our son went into the Air Force and was stationed in Alaska, he traveled and explored that huge state as often as he could get time off, because traveling was a value he considered important.

We have also made it a point to travel outside of the U.S. through the years, which has greatly enlarged and expanded us. But none of these trips came about as a spur of the moment event. We had to pray about it, get the vision for it, set travel as a high value, make some plans, set aside some finances, set our calendar, etc.

You might ask, "Didn't that cost some money and take a lot of time?" Well, sure it did. But we have found that if you line up your life with God's plan, and then submit all you do into His hands, then He always provides all you need, when you need it. We have never had a large income over the years but we have experienced things and traveled places that are way beyond what it seemed we could afford.

There is another great passage in the book of Proverbs about planning, which says, "Lazy people should learn a lesson from the way ants live. They have no leader, chief, or ruler, but they store up their food during the summer, getting ready for winter. How long is the lazy man going to lie around? When is he going to ever get up? 'I'll just take a short nap,' he says; 'I'll fold my hands and rest awhile.' But while he sleeps, poverty will attack him like an armed robber." (Prov. 6: 6-11 GNT)[33]

The lowly ant appears here to be wiser than many of us human beings. They have enough foresight to store up food when it is available and then set it aside for the times when no food is available. Therefore, when winter comes they have plenty while many other insects die from starvation. The result of not planning is described graphically as an armed robber. Most people would take great care to avoid being robbed by a thief, yet this passage tells us that lack of planning is just like being robbed by a thief!

We have read a number of books and articles over the years and have borrowed and adapted many principles from them. In addition to that, we have developed our own tools and ideas that have worked well for our family. Each of you will need to take what you can use from others and adapt it to your own way of doing things. I have worked with many people in a counseling setting and have observed a lot of different methods that work to achieve the same goal.

---

[33] Holy Bible. Proverbs 6:6-11. Good News Translation (GNT).

What does this look like at our house?

Let us share with you how we go about making a plan for the calendar year. Every family will do things a little differently, but there should be some basic principles and ideas here that you can use for yourself. We will share some of the things we have found helpful so you can get some ideas about how you might structure your planning process. Be sure that you can block out at least a half day (a whole day is better) and go to a place where you will not be interrupted. Having a series of uninterrupted meetings over several days works well, too.

We usually **set the date** for our family meeting for early January. We start off with prayer, thanking the Lord for His blessings for the past year and committing the upcoming year into His hands. Then we look back at the past year and discuss it before looking ahead to the future.

So the first part of our yearly meeting is dedicated to looking at the **past year** to see how things went. After we review the past year, we move along to the notes we made at the similar meeting one year earlier, looking to see if we fulfilled last year's goals and if we stayed true to our life's vision. There are always some things on our list that we did not accomplish, as well as goals that we did accomplish. Some of last year's unreached goals can be added to the list of goals for the upcoming year.

We have found it to be very helpful to also write down and discuss the results in several other areas from the previous year which have had an impact upon our lives. Here is a list of what we have used in our family:

1. Key events of the year

2. Key people who have blessed us

3. Key provisions

4. Our travels

5. Impacting books, movies, teachings, or articles we have read

6. Successes

7. Failures/disappointments

8. New friendships developed

9. Trials and tests

10. Key revelations

11. Offenses incurred/inflicted

12. Family themes/seasons of life

Then we work on planning and establishing goals for the **new year**. We review our beliefs, vision, and values first. Visions and values are not stagnant and rigid; they are living and developing. Therefore we find that they will tend to expand and develop as we continue on our journey through life.

Before we ever start making goals for the new year, we should check to see if there are some things we were doing last year that need to be ended. Maybe something was good for the past but now it is time for it to come to an end. It is sometimes hard to end activities that we have been doing for a while, but it is important for us to be good stewards of our time, and our time should be budgeted just as our finances are budgeted. There is a time to say "no" to things that need to be ended.

The busyness of our American culture is one of the biggest hindrances to a fulfilling life. It is so easy to get caught up in the frantic pace of daily life and lose track of who you are and where you are going. As you grow in true wisdom you will learn to weed out activities that will rob you of time and energy. That is a good reason for you to start learning when to say "no".

Now we can begin to hammer out a plan for the new year. **Goals** should always be in harmony with our **beliefs, vision**, and

values. If they are not, they should be tossed out. It is also very important to endeavor to have family unity and agreement in all these different aspects.

As far as the timing of things, we have found it very helpful to break our goal-setting into two categories. First we set our **short-term goals**. By that we mean anything that we feel we can expect to accomplish within one year. And after that we look at the **long-term goals**, those being anything that will probably take longer than a year.

In addition to the short-term/ long-term breakdown, we again divide our goals up into **financial goals** and **non-financial goals**. It just seems to help us to focus better using this type of separation. So by using these two breakdowns we end up with four types of goals for the family.

This whole planning process is not complicated, but it can be challenging. It takes prayer and concentrated thinking to come up with meaningful content. If it comes too easily then you might not really be taking the process seriously. Finding God's will and fulfilling it will cost you, but the rewards for such work are well worth it.

The point is this: in order to come up with some effective goals, you must look at a lot of factors so that the goals don't end up being just a whim or a fancy. Goals that are really unattainable will simply bring frustration. Goals that are shallow and easily reached will leave you unsatisfied and underachieving.

Don't be afraid to dream!

There is a final part of this yearly meeting that can be a lot of fun. We like to keep a list of our **life dreams**.... the desires and wishes that we have in the depth of our heart. While thinking and working on this step we need to remember that there is no limit to what is allowed.

Everyone should be in touch with their dreams because sometimes God is the One who puts dreams in our hearts. Now by nature a dream is often something that you probably could never experience by natural means and efforts. But God is the God of the impossible. And we have found by experience that He loves to plant dreams in hearts and then bring them to pass, just to show Himself as a loving and outrageously generous Father!

Let us say one more thing about dreams. Yes, we should be very serious about accomplishing great things in life. But there is also a place for things that are just plain fun! So dreams don't always have to be about the business of life. They can be about things that simply bring delight to our hearts.

So don't be afraid to write down dreams you might have. We are not saying they will all come to pass, but God may have plans concerning your dreams that you don't know about. Just hold onto them loosely, and allow for the impossible that could happen! You can relax. God knows if any of your dreams would not be good for you and those around you, and He will never lead you into anything like that.

So this is a look at what we do at our yearly family meeting. But it doesn't stop there. During the year at appropriate times (maybe the 6- month point) it is important to take out the notes from your meeting and review them. Be sure that you are taking the actual steps to fulfill those goals and plans. Be sure that you are staying true to your beliefs, vision, and values. And take the time to re-orient yourself if you have started to drift away from the path you have laid out.

Don't forget - this process is not rigid and plans can be changed. Yes, you might have to make adjustments during the year. But even if you do, you should be careful to stay aligned with your vision. God can always give you new insight that might require an adjustment to the plans you have made.

We have also found it fulfilling to look back at the notes from meetings of past years. Once goals are achieved they are dropped from the next year's plan. This is why we like to keep notes from past years, so that from time to time we can look back and see how God blessed and provided in those years. You will be amazed as you see how God has been leading you and providing for you in ways you would never have imagined!

The challenge

Setting goals is one of the most challenging steps in this whole process, for if there are no goals, a person never has to worry about failing or not measuring up! He will never fall short of his goals because he has none. Setting goals forces us into the process of making some progress toward those goals, which requires us to do some work.

The trend in today's society is to live for today, or "fly by the seat of your pants." As the world drifts farther and farther from God, people seem to want to live a more self-centered life. Life has lost meaning for so many in our society, and having goals and plans is a foreign concept for them. If life is meaningless, or just lived for the pleasures of the moment, why should anyone need to plan for the future?

Living in and for the present seems to be good at the time. But at the end of your life you will want to be able to look back and be happy with your accomplishments, with how you've lived, with who you've become. Those who neglect to make plans and set goals will probably have little to show for their lives. God wants us to be those whose lives are full of fruitfulness and accomplishment!

Section 6:

Legacy

"Behold, I am going to send you Elijah the prophet before the coming of the great and terrible day of the LORD. He will restore the hearts of the fathers to their children and the hearts of the children to their fathers, so that I will not come and smite the land with a curse."
Malachi 4:5-6 (NASB)[34]

What a wonderful promise God made in the last two verses of the Old Testament, to bring a restoration of relationships. He did this by sending His own Son into the world to take away the curse of sin and replace it with the blessing of God. First and foremost He restored the relationship between Himself and people. In addition, He also provided for the restoration of the relationship between parents and children.

Jesus took away the legacy of broken relationships within the fallen race of mankind, a legacy of sin and destruction, and replaced it with the legacy of love and blessings. He wants this new heritage to start in the family - one of parents leaving a godly inheritance to their children.

---

[34] Holy Bible. Malachi 4:5-6. New American Standard (NASB).

57

Through this *User's Guide* we have shared with you some tools that we believe will help you find and fulfill the destiny God has for your life. But this is not just for you; it is also for you to help other people do the same.

How wonderful would it be for parents to prepare their children for life, so that by the time they leave home they are already on their way to a fulfilling and abundant life! This will not happen by chance. It will have to be something the parents live out themselves and then intentionally train their children to live out as well.

God will give parents the insights and ability to know each child's strengths and giftings /talents, along with a good idea of how to prepare them for life. With this understanding parents will be able to lay the foundation the children need to find and fulfill their destiny. The atmosphere and culture of the home will have a profound impact not only on how children develop but whether they will be prepared to live a fulfilling life.

Healthy values should be instilled in a child from an early age. The values of the family will most likely be the most important influence on the children. Strong values such as love for God and people, respect, honesty, obedience, kindness, selflessness, responsibility, humility, purity, etc., are vital to the healthy maturing of a child. When values are not taught and exemplified at home, children will pick them up at school or in the neighborhood, and most people would agree that if this happens, things will not end up well.

Every child is born with the desire to be valued, to be significant, and to have a purpose in life. These things need to be nurtured and affirmed by the parents. The family is like a greenhouse where young plants can be protected, nourished, and matured. Then they can be safely transplanted out into the world, secure in who they are, prepared and equipped to pursue a happy and fruitful life.

Dr. Ben Carson

Dr. Ben Carson's life is a great example of the importance a successful parent plays in the life of a child. Ben's mother, Sonya (a single mom), raised her family in a poor Detroit neighborhood. She instilled godly vision and values in Ben, and encouraged him daily. The training and preparation she provided enabled him to eventually become a most excellent pediatric neurosurgeon and also a wonderful example of a godly man. Although Sonya (one of 24 siblings) dropped out of school in the third grade in Tennessee, and bounced around between foster homes, she was determined to help her son (who struggled in elementary school) to get an education and succeed in life. Ben, in turn, has quite a legacy to pass on to many.

So what we have put together in the *User's Guide* can affect many more people than just you, the reader. You have the opportunity and responsibility to leave a godly legacy, which we believe should include passing along these life skills to those in your family and beyond your family as well. What kind of legacy will you leave?

May God bless you as you seek to find and fulfill YOUR destiny!

"Now may the God of peace- who brought up from the dead our Lord Jesus, the great Shepherd of the sheep, and ratified an eternal covenant with his blood- may he equip you with all you need for doing his will.

May he produce in you, through the power of Jesus Christ, every good thing that is pleasing to him.

All glory to him forever and ever! Amen!"

Hebrews 13:20-21 (NLT). [35]

---

[35] Holy Bible. Hebrews 13:20-21. New Living Translation (NLT)

Appendix:
Personal Belief Statement

After reading the first section called Identity, you may wonder what a person's set of central beliefs look like when written out. I think a good example of a personal belief statement is what you might see listed as the belief statement of a good Bible-believing church. The core belief statement of an individual should cover basically the same areas.

Here is a list of some of the essential components which we believe should be found in a solid Biblical belief statement:

1. Something about the person and nature of God

2. Something about the Bible, its origin, and its infallibility

3. Something about mankind, his origin and condition

4. Something about the universe, its creation, its origin, and what sustains it

5. Something about sin, the gospel, and salvation

6. Something about the Kingdom of God and its present- day workings

7. Something about death, the resurrection of the dead, and eternal judgment

8. Something about the return of Jesus Christ to the earth

9. Something about the end of all things as we now know them and about the new heaven and new earth to come

It is very important for every person to write out his own belief statement.   When we wrote ours we just took a few belief statements from several churches that we respect for their solid Bible-based teaching. We read them over and took some from each of these statements for our personal statements. And we also changed the wording in minor ways to make our statement more down to earth and understandable, and applicable to us personally.

Since everything we do in life springs out of what we believe, it is very important to take the time to clearly spell out what you believe. The following statement is one that we use for our family.

Central Belief Statement- Personal

God
There is one God, infinite in glory, wisdom, holiness, justice, power, and love, one in His essence, but eternally substantial in Three Persons: Father, Son, and Holy Spirit.

Father
God the Father is the Creator of heaven and earth. By His Word and for His glory, He freely and supernaturally created the world out of nothing. By the same Word He daily sustains all His creatures. He rules over all and is the only Sovereign. His plans and purposes cannot be thwarted. He is faithful to every promise, works all things together for good to those who love Him, and in His

unfathomable grace gave His Son Jesus Christ for mankind's redemption. He made man for fellowship with Himself, and intended that all creation should live to the praise of His glory. He is the First Person of the Trinity.

Jesus Christ

Jesus Christ, the only begotten Son of God, was the eternal Word made flesh, supernaturally conceived by the Holy Spirit, born of the Virgin Mary. He is perfect in nature, teaching, and obedience. He is fully God and fully man. He was always with God and is God. Through Him all things came into being and were created. He was before all things and in Him all things hold together by the word of His power. He is the image of the invisible God, the firstborn of all creation, and in Him dwells the fullness of the Godhead bodily. He is the only Savior for the sins of the world, having shed His blood and having died a vicarious death on Calvary's cross. By His death in our place, He revealed the divine love and upheld divine justice, removing our guilt and reconciling us to God. Having redeemed us from sin, the third day He rose bodily from the grave, victorious over death and the powers of darkness, and for a period of forty days appeared to over five hundred witnesses performing many convincing proofs of His resurrection. He ascended into heaven where, at God's right hand, He intercedes for His people and rules as Lord over all. He is the Head of His body the Church, and should be adored, loved, served, and obeyed by all. He is the Second Person of the Trinity.

The Holy Spirit

The Holy Spirit, the Lord and Giver of life, convicts the world of sin, righteousness and judgment. Through the proclamation of the gospel He persuades men to repent of their sins and confess Jesus Christ as Lord. By the same Spirit a person is led to trust in His divine mercy. The Holy Spirit unites believers to Jesus Christ in faith, brings about the new birth, and dwells within the regenerate. The Holy Spirit has come to glorify the Son who in turn came to glorify the Father. He will lead the Church into a right understanding and rich application of God's Word. He is to be respected, honored, and worshiped as God, the Third Person of the Trinity.

The Bible

We accept the Bible, including the 39 books of the Old Testament and the 27 books of the New Testament, as the written Word of God. The Bible is the only essential and infallible record of God's self-disclosure to mankind. Being given by God, the Scriptures are both fully and verbally inspired by God.

Therefore, as originally given, the Bible is free of error in all it teaches. Each book is to be interpreted according to its context and purpose and in reverent obedience to the Lord who speaks through it in living power. All believers are exhorted to study the Scriptures and diligently apply them to their lives. The Scriptures are the authoritative and normative rule and guide of all Christian life, practices, and doctrine. They are totally sufficient and must not be added to, superseded, or changed by later tradition, extra-biblical revelation, or worldly wisdom. Every doctrinal formulation, whether of creed, confession, or theology, must be put to the test of the full counsel of God in Holy Scripture.

Creation

God sovereignly created the world out of nothing by His spoken word, and also upholds, sustains, governs, and providentially directs all that exists. The universe did not evolve to its present state on its own or by chance but was created by God.

Creation of Man

God created man in His own image, in a state of original righteousness, from which he subsequently fell by voluntary revolt, and as a consequence is guilty, inherently corrupt, and subject to divine wrath. The unregenerate man is totally depraved and does not possess a will free from the dominion of the sin nature.

The Gospel

Jesus Christ is the gospel. The good news is revealed in His birth, life, death, resurrection and ascension. Christ's crucifixion is the heart of the gospel, His resurrection is the power of the gospel, and His ascension is the glory of the gospel. Christ's death is the substitutionary and propitiatory sacrifice to God for our sins. It satisfies the demands of God's holy justice and appeases His holy wrath. It also demonstrates His mysterious love and reveals His amazing grace. Jesus Christ is the only mediator between God and man. There is no other name by which men must be saved. At the heart of all sound doctrine are the Cross of Jesus Christ and the infinite privilege that redeemed sinners have of glorifying God because of what He has accomplished. Therefore, we want all that takes place in our hearts, churches, and ministries to proceed from and be related to the Cross.

Salvation

Salvation consists of the remission of sins, the impartation of the righteousness of Jesus Christ, the gift of eternal life, and the blessings that accompany these, which are a free gift of God, and received by faith alone apart from human works of merit. Even the ability to believe is a gift of God. This blessing in no way relieves men of their responsibility to repent and believe. After repentance toward God and faith toward the Lord Jesus Christ, the believer is to publicly proclaim his identity with Christ by immersion in water baptism, in the name of the Father, Son, and Holy Spirit.

Empowering by the Spirit

In addition to effecting regeneration and sanctification, the Holy Spirit also empowers believers for Christian witness and service. While all genuine believers are indwelt by the Holy Spirit at conversion, the New Testament indicates the importance of an ongoing, empowering work of the Spirit subsequent to conversion as well. Being indwelt by the Spirit and being filled with the Spirit are theologically distinct experiences. The Holy Spirit desires to fill each believer continually with increased power for Christian life and witness, and imparts his supernatural gifts for the edification of the Body and for various works of ministry in the world. All the gifts of the Holy Spirit at work in the church of the first century are available today, are vital for the mission of the church, and are to be earnestly desired and practiced.

The Return of Jesus Christ and the Consummation of All Things

The Consummation of all things includes the visible, personal, and glorious return of Jesus Christ, the resurrection of the dead, and the translation of those alive in Christ, the judgment of the just and the unjust, and the fulfillment of Christ's Kingdom in the new heavens and the new earth. In the Consummation, Satan and his demonic hosts and all those who are not in Christ will be finally separated from the benevolent presence of God, enduring eternal punishment. But the righteous, in resurrected and glorified bodies, shall live and reign with Him forever. Married to Christ as His Bride, the Church will be in the presence of God forever, serving Him and giving Him unending praise and glory. Then shall the eager expectation of creation be fulfilled, and the whole earth shall proclaim the glory of God who makes all things new.

The first heaven and earth will completely pass away and the new Jerusalem will come down from heaven prepared as a pure bride for her husband. The dwelling of God will be with mankind and they will live with God forever!

Made in the USA
Middletown, DE
17 March 2025

72811737R00037